Table of Contents

Soups & Stews

Fresh Lime and Black Bean Soup

- 2 cans (about 15 ounces each) black beans, undrained
- 1 can (about 14 ounces) chicken broth
- 1½ cups chopped onions
- 1½ teaspoons chili powder
- ¾ teaspoon ground cumin
- ¼ teaspoon garlic powder
- ⅛ to ¼ teaspoon red pepper flakes
- ½ cup sour cream
- 2 tablespoons chopped fresh cilantro
- 2 tablespoons extra-virgin olive oil
- 1 medium lime, cut into wedges

Slow Cooker Directions

1. Coat slow cooker with nonstick cooking spray. Add beans, broth, onions, chili powder, cumin, garlic powder and pepper flakes. Cover; cook on LOW 7 hours or on HIGH 3½ hours.

2. Process 1 cup soup mixture in blender until smooth and return to slow cooker. Stir and check consistency; repeat with additional 1 cup soup, if desired. Let stand 15 to 20 minutes before serving.

3. Ladle soup into bowls. Top with sour cream, cilantro and oil. Squeeze juice from lime wedges over each.   *Makes 4 servings*

Prep Time: 10 minutes
Cook Time: 7 hours (LOW) or 3½ hours (HIGH)

Louisiana Gumbo

    2 cups MINUTE® White Rice, uncooked
    2 tablespoons butter
    2 tablespoons all-purpose flour
    ½ cup chopped onion
    ½ cup chopped celery
    ½ cup chopped green bell pepper
    1 clove garlic, minced
    1 package (14 ounces) smoked turkey sausage, sliced
    1 can (14½ ounces) diced tomatoes
    1 can (14½ ounces) condensed chicken broth
    1 package (10 ounces) frozen sliced okra, thawed*
    1 tablespoon Cajun seasoning
    ¼ teaspoon dried thyme
    ½ pound shrimp, peeled, deveined
      Salt and black pepper, to taste

Or substitute 1 package (10 ounces) frozen cut green beans.

Prepare rice according to package directions. Melt butter in large skillet over medium-high heat. Stir in flour; cook and stir until light golden brown, about 5 minutes. Add onion, celery, bell pepper and garlic; cook 2 to 3 minutes or until tender. Stir in sausage, tomatoes, broth, okra, seasoning and thyme; cover. Simmer 5 minutes, stirring occasionally. Add shrimp; cook 5 minutes or until shrimp are pink. Season with salt and pepper to taste. Serve with rice.   *Makes 6 servings*

Pizza Soup

    2 cans (about 14 ounces each) stewed tomatoes with
        Italian seasonings, undrained
    2 cups beef broth
    1 cup sliced mushrooms
    1 small onion, chopped
    1 tablespoon tomato paste
    ¼ teaspoon salt
    ¼ teaspoon black pepper
    ½ pound turkey Italian sausage, casings removed
      Shredded mozzarella cheese

continued on page 6

Pizza Soup, continued

Slow Cooker Directions
1. Combine tomatoes with juice, broth, mushrooms, onion, tomato paste, salt and pepper in slow cooker.

2. Shape sausage into balls. Gently stir into soup mixture. Cover; cook on LOW 6 to 7 hours. Sprinkle with cheese.   *Makes 4 servings*

Prep Time: 10 minutes
Cook Time: 6 to 7 hours

Hearty Chicken Chili

   1 **medium onion, finely chopped**
   1 **small jalapeño pepper,* cored, seeded and minced**
   1 **clove garlic, minced**
1½ **teaspoons chili powder**
  ¾ **teaspoon salt**
  ½ **teaspoon black pepper**
  ½ **teaspoon ground cumin**
  ½ **teaspoon dried oregano**
  ¼ **teaspoon red pepper flakes (optional)**
1½ **pounds boneless skinless chicken thighs, cut into 1-inch pieces**
   2 **cans (about 15 ounces each) hominy, rinsed and drained**
   1 **can (about 15 ounces) pinto beans, rinsed and drained**
   1 **cup chicken broth**
   1 **tablespoon all-purpose flour (optional)**
    Chopped fresh parsley or fresh cilantro (optional)

*Jalapeño peppers can sting and irritate the skin, so wear rubber gloves when handling peppers and do not touch eyes.

Slow Cooker Directions
1. Combine onion, jalapeño, garlic, chili powder, salt, black pepper, cumin, oregano and pepper flakes, if desired, in slow cooker.

2. Add chicken, hominy, beans and broth. Stir well to combine. Cover; cook on LOW 7 hours.

3. If thicker gravy is desired, combine 1 tablespoon flour and 3 tablespoons cooking liquid in small bowl. Add to slow cooker. Cover; cook on HIGH 10 minutes or until thickened. Serve in bowls and garnish with parsley.   *Makes 6 servings*

Prep Time: 15 minutes
Cook Time: 7 hours (LOW), plus 10 minutes (HIGH)

Italian Mushroom Soup

1½ **cups boiling water**
½ **cup dried porcini mushrooms (about ½ ounce)**
1 **tablespoon olive oil**
2 **cups chopped onions**
8 **ounces sliced cremini or button mushrooms**
2 **cloves garlic, minced**
¼ **teaspoon dried thyme**
¼ **cup all-purpose flour**
4 **cups chicken or vegetable broth**
½ **cup whipping cream**
½ **teaspoon black pepper**

1. Combine boiling water and porcini mushrooms in small bowl; let stand 15 to 20 minutes or until mushrooms are tender.

2. Meanwhile, heat oil in large saucepan over medium heat. Add onions; cook 5 minutes or until translucent, stirring occasionally. Add cremini mushrooms, garlic and thyme; cook 8 minutes, stirring occasionally. Add flour; cook and stir 1 minute. Stir in broth.

3. Drain porcini mushrooms, reserving liquid. Chop mushrooms; add mushrooms and reserved liquid to saucepan. Bring to a boil over high heat. Reduce heat; simmer 10 minutes. Stir in cream and pepper. Simmer 5 minutes or until heated through. Serve immediately.   *Makes 6 to 8 servings*

Jerk Pork and Sweet Potato Stew

  2 tablespoons all-purpose flour
  ¼ teaspoon salt
  ¼ teaspoon black pepper
1¼ pounds pork shoulder, cut into bite-size pieces
  2 tablespoons vegetable oil
  1 large sweet potato, peeled and diced
  1 cup corn
  ¼ cup minced green onions, divided
  1 clove garlic, minced
  ½ medium scotch bonnet chile or jalapeño pepper,* cored, seeded and
      minced
  ⅛ teaspoon ground allspice
  1 cup chicken broth
  1 tablespoon lime juice

Scotch bonnet chiles and jalapeño peppers can sting and irritate the skin, so wear rubber gloves when handling and do not touch your eyes.

Slow Cooker Directions

1. Combine flour, salt and black pepper in large resealable food storage bag. Add pork; shake well to coat. Heat oil in large skillet over medium heat. Working in batches, add pork in single layer and brown on all sides, about 5 minutes. Transfer to 4- or 5-quart slow cooker.

2. Add sweet potato, corn, 2 tablespoons green onions, garlic, chile and allspice. Stir in broth. Cover; cook on LOW 5 to 6 hours.

3. Stir in lime juice and remaining 2 tablespoons green onions.   *Makes 4 servings*

Spicy Squash & Chicken Soup

  1 tablespoon vegetable oil
  1 small onion, finely chopped
  1 stalk celery, finely chopped
  2 cups butternut squash (1 small squash), cut into 1-inch cubes
  2 cups chicken broth
  1 can (about 14 ounces) diced tomatoes, undrained
  1 cup chopped cooked chicken
  ½ teaspoon ground ginger
  ¼ teaspoon salt
  ⅛ teaspoon *each* ground cumin and black pepper
  2 teaspoons fresh lime juice
  1 tablespoon minced fresh cilantro (optional)

1. Heat oil in large saucepan over medium heat. Add onion and celery; cook and stir 5 minutes or just until tender. Stir in squash, broth, tomatoes, chicken, ginger, salt, cumin and pepper; mix well.

2. Cover and cook over low heat 30 minutes or until squash is tender. Stir in lime juice. Sprinkle with cilantro. *Makes 4 servings*

Variation: For an extra-spicy soup, use diced tomatoes with chiles.

Baked Potato Soup

- ¼ **cup (½ stick) butter or margarine**
- ¼ **cup chopped onion**
- ¼ **cup all-purpose flour**
- 1 **can (14½ fluid ounces) chicken broth**
- 1 **can (12 fluid ounces) NESTLÉ® CARNATION® Evaporated Milk**
- 2 **large or 3 medium baking potatoes, baked or microwaved**
  Cooked and crumbled bacon (optional)
  Shredded Cheddar cheese (optional)
  Sliced green onions (optional)

Melt butter in large saucepan over medium heat. Add onion; cook, stirring occasionally, for 1 to 2 minutes or until tender. Stir in flour. Gradually stir in broth and evaporated milk. Scoop potato pulp from 1 potato (reserve potato skin); mash. Add pulp to broth mixture. Cook over medium heat, stirring occasionally, until mixture comes to a boil. Dice remaining potato skin and potato(es); add to soup. Heat through. Season with salt and ground black pepper. Top each serving with bacon, cheese and green onions, if desired. *Makes 4 servings*

Variation: For a different twist to this recipe, omit the bacon, Cheddar cheese and green onions. Cook 2 tablespoons shredded carrot with the onion and add ¼ teaspoon dried dill to the soup when adding the broth. Proceed as above.

Italian Hillside Garden Soup

1 tablespoon olive oil
1 cup chopped onion
1 cup chopped green bell pepper
½ cup sliced celery
2 cans (about 14 ounces each) chicken broth
1 can (about 14 ounces) diced tomatoes with basil, garlic and oregano
1 can (about 15 ounces) navy beans, drained and rinsed
1 medium zucchini, chopped
1 cup frozen cut green beans, thawed
¼ teaspoon garlic powder
1 package (9 ounces) refrigerated sausage- or cheese-filled tortellini pasta
3 tablespoons chopped fresh basil
Grated Asiago or Parmesan cheese (optional)

Slow Cooker Directions

1. Heat oil in large skillet over medium-high heat. Add onion, bell pepper and celery. Cook and stir 4 minutes or until onions are translucent. Transfer to slow cooker.

2. Add broth, tomatoes, navy beans, zucchini, green beans and garlic powder. Cover; cook on LOW 7 hours or on HIGH 3½ hours.

3. Turn slow cooker to HIGH. Add tortellini and cook 20 to 25 minutes longer or until pasta is tender. Stir in basil. Garnish each serving with cheese.

Makes 6 servings

Prep Time: 15 minutes
Cook Time: 7 hours (LOW) or 3½ hours (HIGH), plus 20 minutes (HIGH)

Asian Beef Stew

1½ **pounds beef round steak, sliced thinly across the grain**
2 **onions, cut into ¼-inch slices**
2 **stalks celery, sliced**
2 **carrots, peeled and sliced** *or* **1 cup peeled baby carrots**
1 **cup sliced mushrooms**
1 **cup orange juice**
1 **cup beef broth**
⅓ **cup hoisin sauce**
2 **tablespoons cornstarch**
1 to 2 **teaspoons Chinese five-spice powder or curry powder**
1 **cup frozen peas**
  Hot cooked rice
  Chopped fresh cilantro (optional)

Slow Cooker Directions

1. Place beef, onions, celery, carrots and mushrooms in slow cooker.

2. Combine orange juice, broth, hoisin sauce, cornstarch and five-spice powder in small bowl. Pour into slow cooker. Cover; cook on HIGH 5 hours.

3. Stir in peas. Cook 20 minutes or until peas are tender. Serve with hot cooked rice. Garnish with cilantro. *Makes 6 servings*

Prep Time: 10 minutes
Cook Time: 5 hours, 20 minutes

Hearty Vegetable Stew

1 **tablespoon olive oil**
1 **cup chopped onion**
¾ **cup chopped carrots**
3 **cloves garlic, minced**
4 **cups coarsely chopped green cabbage**
3½ **cups coarsely chopped red potatoes (about 3 medium)**
1 **teaspoon** *each* **salt and dried rosemary**
½ **teaspoon black pepper**
4 **cups vegetable broth**
1 **can (about 15 ounces) Great Northern Beans, rinsed and drained**
1 **can (about 14 ounces) diced tomatoes**
  Grated Parmesan cheese (optional)

continued on page 16

Hearty Vegetable Stew, continued

1. Heat oil in large saucepan over high heat. Add onion and carrots; cook and stir 3 minutes. Add garlic; cook and stir 1 minute.

2. Add cabbage, potatoes, salt, rosemary and pepper; cook 1 minute. Stir in broth, beans and tomatoes; bring to a boil. Reduce heat to medium-low; simmer about 15 minutes or until potatoes are tender. Sprinkle with cheese.

Makes about 7 servings

Italian Sausage Soup

Sausage Meatballs

    1 pound mild Italian sausage, casings removed
    ½ cup plain dry bread crumbs
    ¼ cup grated Parmesan cheese
    ¼ cup milk
    1 egg
    ½ teaspoon dried basil
    ½ teaspoon black pepper
    ¼ teaspoon garlic salt

Soup

    4 cups chicken broth
    1 tablespoon tomato paste
    1 clove garlic, minced
    ¼ teaspoon red pepper flakes
    ½ cup mini shell pasta*
    1 bag (10 ounces) baby spinach
    Grated Parmesan cheese

Or use other tiny pasta such as ditalini (mini tubes) or farfallini (mini bowties).

Slow Cooker Directions

1. Combine all meatball ingredients in large bowl. Form into balls.

2. Combine broth, tomato paste, garlic and pepper flakes in slow cooker. Add meatballs. Cover; cook on LOW 5 to 6 hours.

3. Add pasta; cook on LOW 30 minutes or until pasta is tender. Stir in spinach. Ladle into bowls; sprinkle with cheese and serve immediately.   *Makes 4 to 6 servings*

Prep Time: 15 minutes
Cook Time: 5 to 6 hours

Green Chile Chicken Soup with Tortilla Dumplings

  8 ORTEGA® Taco Shells, broken
  ½ cup water
  ⅓ cup milk
  2 onions, diced, divided
  1 egg
  ½ teaspoon POLANER® Minced Garlic
  1 tablespoon olive oil
  4 cups chicken broth
  2 cups shredded cooked chicken
  2 tablespoons ORTEGA® Roasted Chiles
  ¼ cup vegetable oil

Place taco shells, water, milk, 1 diced onion, egg and garlic in blender or food processor. Pulse several times to crush taco shells and blend ingredients. Pour into medium bowl; let stand 10 minutes to thicken.

Heat 1 tablespoon olive oil in saucepan over medium heat. Add remaining diced onion; cook and stir 4 minutes or until translucent. Stir in broth, chicken and chiles. Reduce heat to a simmer.

Heat ¼ cup oil in small skillet over medium heat. Form taco shell mixture into 1-inch balls. Drop into hot oil in batches. Cook dumplings about 3 minutes or until browned. Turn over and continue cooking 3 minutes longer or until browned. Remove dumplings; drain on paper towels. Add dumplings to soup just before serving.

Makes 4 to 6 servings

Prep Time: 15 minutes
Start to Finish: 30 minutes

 Tip   For an even more authentic Mexican flavor, garnish the soup with fresh chopped cilantro and a squirt of lime juice.

Green Chile Chicken Soup with Tortilla Dumplings

Savory Breads

Three-Grain Bread

 1 cup whole wheat flour
 ¾ cup all-purpose flour
 1 package rapid-rise active dry yeast
 1 cup milk
 2 tablespoons honey
 1 tablespoon olive oil
 1 teaspoon salt
 ½ cup old-fashioned oats
 ¼ cup whole grain cornmeal plus additional for baking sheet
 1 egg beaten with 1 tablespoon water (optional)
 1 tablespoon old-fashioned oats for topping (optional)

1. Combine whole wheat flour, all-purpose flour and yeast in large bowl. Stir milk, honey, olive oil and salt in small saucepan over low heat until warm (110° to 120°F). Stir milk mixture into flour; beat 3 minutes with electric mixer at high speed. Mix in oats and cornmeal at low speed. If dough is too wet, add additional flour by teaspoonfuls until it begins to come together.

2. Turn dough out onto floured surface and knead 8 minutes or until dough is smooth and elastic. Place dough in large, lightly oiled bowl; turn once to coat. Cover; let rise in warm place (85°F) about 1 hour or until dough is puffy and does not spring back when touched.

3. Punch dough down and shape into 8-inch long loaf. Place on baking sheet lightly dusted with cornmeal. Cover; let rise in warm place until almost doubled, about 45 minutes. Meanwhile, preheat oven to 375°F.

4. Make shallow slash down center of loaf with sharp knife. Brush lightly with egg mixture and sprinkle with oats, if desired. Bake 30 minutes or until loaf sounds hollow when tapped (internal temperature of 200°F). Remove to wire rack to cool.

Makes 1 loaf

Sage Buns

1½ **cups milk**
2 **tablespoons shortening**
3 **to 4 cups all-purpose flour, divided**
2 **tablespoons sugar**
1 **package active dry yeast**
2 **teaspoons rubbed sage**
1 **teaspoon salt**
1 **tablespoon olive oil (optional)**

1. Heat milk and shortening in small saucepan over medium heat, stirring constantly, until shortening is melted and temperature reaches 110°F to 120°F. Remove from heat.

2. Combine 2 cups flour, sugar, yeast, sage and salt in large bowl. Add milk mixture; beat vigorously 2 minutes. Add remaining flour, ¼ cup at a time, until dough begins to pull away from sides of bowl.

3. Turn dough out onto floured surface; flatten slightly. Knead 10 minutes or until dough is smooth and elastic, adding flour, if necessary, to prevent sticking.

4. Shape dough into ball. Place dough in large, lightly oiled bowl; turn once to coat. Cover; let rise in warm place (85°F) 1 hour or until doubled. Grease 13×9-inch pan; set aside.

5. Turn dough out onto lightly oiled surface. Divide into 24 equal pieces. Form each piece into ball. Space evenly in prepared pan. Cover; let rise 45 minutes.

6. Preheat oven to 375°F. Bake 15 to 20 minutes or until golden brown. Immediately remove bread from pan and cool on wire rack. Brush tops of rolls with olive oil for soft, shiny tops, if desired.   *Makes 24 rolls*

Easy Cheesy Bacon Bread

  1 pound sliced bacon, chopped
  1 onion, chopped
  1 green bell pepper, chopped
  ½ teaspoon ground red pepper
  3 cans (7½ ounces each) refrigerated buttermilk biscuits
2½ cups (10 ounces) shredded Cheddar cheese, divided
  ½ cup (1 stick) butter, melted

1. Preheat oven to 350°F. Spray nonstick bundt pan with nonstick cooking spray. Cook bacon in large skillet over medium heat about 4 minutes or until crisp. Remove bacon with slotted spoon to paper towels. Reserve 1 tablespoon drippings in skillet. Add onion, bell pepper and red pepper; cook and stir over medium-high heat about 10 minutes or until tender. Cool.

2. Cut biscuits into quarters. Combine biscuit pieces, bacon, onion mixture, 2 cups cheese and butter in large bowl; mix gently. Loosely press mixture in prepared pan.

3. Bake 30 minutes or until golden brown. Cool 5 minutes in pan on wire rack. Invert onto serving platter and sprinkle with remaining ½ cup cheese. Serve warm.

Makes 12 servings

Sonoma Dried Tomato and Vegetable Biscuits

  ¼ cup SONOMA® Dried Tomato Halves
2½ cups unbleached all-purpose flour
  1 tablespoon sugar
  2 teaspoons baking powder
  2 teaspoons salt
  ½ teaspoon baking soda
  ¼ teaspoon black pepper
  ½ teaspoon active dry yeast
  2 tablespoons warm water (110° to 115°F)
  1 cup cold vegetable shortening, cut into ½-inch cubes
  ½ cup vegetables, cut into ¼-inch cubes (carrot, yellow squash, green bell pepper and zucchini)
  2 teaspoons *each* fresh minced parsley, basil and dill *or* 1 scant teaspoon *each* dried parsley, basil and dill
  1 large clove garlic, minced
  ¾ cup buttermilk

continued on page 26

Sonoma Dried Tomato and Vegetable Biscuits, continued

Preheat oven to 375°F. In small bowl, cover tomatoes with boiling water; set aside 10 minutes. In large bowl, mix flour, sugar, baking powder, salt, baking soda and black pepper. In another small bowl, dissolve yeast in warm water; set aside. Cut shortening into flour mixture until crumbs resemble coarse meal. Blend yeast mixture into flour mixture to form dough. Thoroughly drain and mince tomatoes; combine with vegetables, herbs and garlic. Add half the vegetable mixture and half the buttermilk to the dough; mix well and repeat with remaining vegetable mixture and buttermilk. Turn dough out onto floured surface and knead several times, adding more flour only if necessary. Pat or roll out dough to ¾-inch thickness; cut out dough with 3-inch biscuit cutter. Place biscuits, spaced 2 inches apart, on greased or parchment-lined baking sheet. Bake 20 to 24 minutes until lightly browned and cooked through.

Makes 8 biscuits

Honey Whole Grain Bread

  3 cups whole wheat flour, divided
  2 cups warm (110° to 120°F) whole milk
  ¾ to 1 cup all-purpose flour, divided
  ¼ cup honey
  2 tablespoons vegetable oil
  1 package (¼ ounce) active dry yeast
  ¾ teaspoon salt

Slow Cooker Directions

1. Spray 1-quart casserole, soufflé dish or other high-sided baking pan that fits into 4½-quart slow cooker with nonstick cooking spray. Combine 1½ cups whole wheat flour, milk, ½ cup all-purpose flour, honey, oil, yeast and salt in large bowl. Beat with electric mixer at medium speed 2 minutes.

2. Add remaining 1½ cups whole wheat flour and ¼ cup to ½ cup all-purpose flour until dough is no longer sticky. (If mixer has difficulty mixing dough, mix in remaining flours with wooden spoon.) Transfer to prepared dish.

3. Make foil handles with strips of heavy-duty foil. Criss-cross 3 or 4 strips and place in slow cooker. Place dish on strips. Cover; cook on HIGH 3 hours or until edges are browned.

4. Use foil handles to lift dish from slow cooker. Let stand 5 minutes. Unmold on wire rack to cool.

Makes 8 to 10 servings

Farmer-Style Sour Cream Bread

    1 cup sour cream, at room temperature
    3 tablespoons water
2½ to 3 cups all-purpose flour, divided
    1 package active dry yeast
    2 tablespoons sugar
1½ teaspoons salt
    ¼ teaspoon baking soda
      Vegetable oil or nonstick cooking spray
    1 tablespoon poppy or sesame seeds

1. Stir together sour cream and water in small saucepan. Heat over low heat until temperature reaches 120° to 130°F. *Do not boil.* Combine 2 cups flour, yeast, sugar, salt and baking soda in large bowl. Stir sour cream mixture into flour mixture until well blended. Turn dough out onto lightly floured surface. Knead about 5 minutes, adding enough remaining flour until dough is smooth and elastic.

2. Grease large baking sheet. Shape dough into ball; place on prepared sheet. Flatten into 8-inch circle. Brush top with oil. Sprinkle with poppy seeds. Invert large bowl over dough and let rise in warm place (85°F) 1 hour or until doubled.

3. Preheat oven to 350°F. Bake 22 to 27 minutes or until golden brown. Remove immediately from baking sheet; cool on wire rack. *Makes 8 to 12 servings*

Roman Meal® Cream of Rye Bread

1¼ teaspoons yeast
  2 cups flour
  ⅔ cup ROMAN MEAL® Cream of Rye Cereal
  2 tablespoons nonfat dry milk
  1 teaspoon salt
  2 teaspoons caraway seeds
  1 tablespoon honey
  2 teaspoons molasses
  2 tablespoons shortening
  1 cup water

Bread Machine Directions
Pour yeast to one side of inner pan. Add remaining ingredients in order. Select white bread and push "start." *Makes 1 loaf*

Roasted Garlic Breadsticks

1 **large head garlic (about 14 to 16 cloves)**
3 **tablespoons olive oil, divided**
3 **tablespoons water, divided**
1 **tablespoon butter or margarine, softened**
1 **cup warm water (110° to 120°F)**
1 **package active dry yeast**
1 **teaspoon sugar**
2½ **to 3 cups all-purpose flour, divided**
1 **teaspoon salt**
1 **egg white**
1 **tablespoon sesame seeds**

1. Preheat oven to 350°F. Remove outer papery skin from garlic. Place garlic in 10-ounce ovenproof custard cup. Drizzle with 1 tablespoon oil and 2 tablespoons water. Cover tightly with foil. Bake 1 hour or until garlic cloves are tender. Remove foil and let cool.

2. When garlic is cool enough to handle, break into cloves. Squeeze skin until garlic pops out. Finely chop garlic cloves. Combine chopped garlic and butter in small bowl. Cover and set aside.

3. Combine 1 cup warm water, yeast and sugar in large bowl; let stand 5 minutes or until bubbly. Beat 1½ cups flour, salt and remaining 2 tablespoons oil into yeast mixture with electric mixer at low speed until blended. Increase speed to medium; beat 2 minutes. Stir in enough additional flour to make soft dough.

4. Turn dough out onto lightly floured surface. Knead about 5 minutes, adding enough remaining flour until dough is smooth and elastic. Shape dough into ball; place in large, lightly oiled bowl. Turn once to coat. Cover; let rise in warm place (85°F) about 1 hour or until doubled.

5. Punch down dough; knead on lightly floured surface 1 minute. Cover; let rest 10 minutes. Grease 2 large baking sheets; set aside. Roll dough into 12-inch square with lightly floured rolling pin. Spread garlic mixture evenly over dough. Fold square in half. Roll dough into 14×7-inch rectangle. Cut dough crosswise into 7×1-inch strips.

6. Holding ends of each strip, twist 3 to 4 times. Place strips 2 inches apart on prepared baking sheets, pressing both ends to seal. Cover; let rise in warm place about 30 minutes or until doubled.

7. Preheat oven to 400°F. Combine egg white and remaining 1 tablespoon water in small bowl. Brush sticks with egg white mixture; sprinkle with sesame seeds. Bake 20 to 22 minutes or until golden. Serve warm.   *Makes 12 breadsticks*

Spicy Cheese Bread

2 packages active dry yeast
1 teaspoon granulated sugar
½ cup warm water (110°F)
8¾ cups flour, divided
3 cups shredded Jarlsberg or Swiss cheese
2 tablespoons fresh chopped rosemary *or* 2 teaspoons dried rosemary
1 tablespoon salt
1 tablespoon Original TABASCO® brand Pepper Sauce
2 cups milk
4 eggs, lightly beaten

Combine yeast, sugar and warm water. Let stand 5 minutes or until foamy. Meanwhile, combine 8 cups flour, cheese, rosemary, salt and TABASCO® Sauce in large bowl. Heat milk in small saucepan until warm (120° to 130°F).

Stir milk into flour mixture. Set aside 1 tablespoon beaten egg. Add remaining eggs to flour mixture with foamy yeast mixture; stir until soft dough forms.

Turn dough out onto lightly floured surface. Knead about 5 minutes, adding enough remaining flour to make a smooth and elastic dough. Shape dough into a ball; place in large greased bowl. Cover with towel and let rise in warm place until doubled, about 1½ hours.

Grease 2 large cookie sheets. Punch down dough and divide in half. Cut each half into 3 strips and braid. Place braided loaves on greased cookie sheets. Cover and let rise in warm place until almost doubled, 30 minutes to 1 hour. Preheat oven to 375°F. Brush loaves with reserved egg. Bake about 45 minutes or until loaves sound hollow when tapped. Remove to wire racks to cool.   *Makes 2 loaves*

English Bath Buns

½ cup warm water (100° to 110°F)
2 envelopes FLEISCHMANN'S® Active Dry Yeast
½ cup warm milk (100° to 110°F)
½ cup (1 stick) butter or margarine, softened
2 tablespoons sugar
1 teaspoon salt
4 cups all-purpose flour
2 eggs
1 egg, lightly beaten with 1 tablespoon water
¼ cup sugar
1 cup chopped almonds

Place warm water in large warm bowl. Sprinkle in yeast; stir until dissolved. Add warm milk, butter, 2 tablespoons sugar, salt and 2 cups flour. Beat 2 minutes at medium speed of electric mixer. Add 2 eggs and ½ cup flour. Beat 2 minutes at high speed, scraping bowl occasionally. Stir in enough remaining flour to make soft dough. Knead on lightly floured surface until smooth and elastic, about 10 minutes. Place in greased bowl, turning to grease top. Cover; let rise in warm, draft-free place until doubled in size, about 1 hour.

Punch dough down; turn out onto lightly floured surface. Divide into 24 equal pieces. Shape each piece into smooth ball. Place in greased 2½-inch muffin cups. Cover; let rise in warm, draft-free place until doubled in size, about 30 minutes. Brush tops with egg mixture. Sprinkle ¼ cup sugar and almonds over tops. Bake at 375°F for 20 minutes or until done. Remove from pans; cool on wire racks.   *Makes 24 buns*

Tip There are several warm places to let dough rise. Place it inside a gas oven warmed by a pilot light or in an electric oven heated to 200°F for 1 minute and then turned off. Your microwave can also be used. Bring 2 cups water to a boil in the microwave, then turn off the power, set the dough inside and close the door.

Main Dishes

Southern Buttermilk Fried Chicken

- 2 cups all-purpose flour
- 1½ teaspoons celery salt
- 1 teaspoon dried thyme
- ¾ teaspoon black pepper
- ½ teaspoon dried marjoram
- 1¾ cups buttermilk
- 2 cups vegetable oil
- 3 pounds chicken pieces

1. Combine flour, celery salt, thyme, pepper and marjoram in shallow bowl. Pour buttermilk into medium bowl.

2. Heat oil in heavy deep skillet over medium heat until 340°F on deep-fry thermometer.

3. Dip chicken in buttermilk, one piece at a time; shake off excess. Coat with flour mixture; shake off excess. Dip again in buttermilk and coat once more with flour mixture. Fry chicken in batches, skin side down, 10 to 12 minutes or until browned. Turn and fry 12 to 14 minutes or until cooked through (165°F). Allow temperature of oil to return to 350°F between batches. Drain chicken on paper towels.

Makes 4 servings

Note: Carefully monitor the temperature of the vegetable oil during cooking. It should not drop below 325°F or go higher than 350°F. The chicken can also be cooked in a deep fryer following the manufacturer's directions. *Never leave hot oil unattended.*

Old-Fashioned Meat Loaf

      1 teaspoon olive oil
      1 cup finely chopped onion
      4 cloves garlic, minced
  1½ pounds ground beef
   ¾ cup old-fashioned oats
      1 cup chili sauce, divided
      2 egg whites
   ½ teaspoon black pepper
   ¼ teaspoon salt (optional)
      1 tablespoon Dijon mustard

1. Preheat oven to 375°F. Heat oil in large nonstick skillet over medium heat. Add onion; cook and stir 5 minutes. Add garlic; cook 1 minute. Remove from heat; transfer to large bowl. Let cool 5 minutes.

2. Add beef, oats, ½ cup chili sauce, egg whites, pepper and salt, if desired; mix well. Shape into loaf; place in 9×5-inch loaf pan. Combine remaining ½ cup chili sauce and mustard in small bowl; spoon evenly over top of meat loaf.

3. Bake 45 to 50 minutes or until internal temperature reaches 160°F. Let stand 5 minutes. Pour off any juices from pan. Cut into slices to serve.

Makes 6 servings

Tuscan Roast Pork Tenderloin

  1⅓ cups French's® French Fried Onions
      1 teaspoon crushed rosemary leaves
   ½ teaspoon garlic powder
   ¼ teaspoon ground black pepper
      1 to 1½ pounds pork tenderloin
      2 tablespoons French's® Spicy Brown Mustard

1. Mix French Fried Onions, rosemary, garlic powder and pepper in plastic bag. Crush with hands or rolling pin.

2. Brush pork with mustard. Coat in seasoned onion crumbs; press firmly to adhere.

3. Bake pork on a foil-lined baking sheet at 400°F for 30 minutes or until internal temperature is 155°F. Let rest 10 minutes before slicing.   *Makes 6 servings*

Tip: Use this savory coating for pork chops or chicken breasts.

Prep Time: 10 minutes
Cook Time: 30 minutes

Oven Barbecue Chicken

1 cup barbecue sauce
¼ cup honey
2 tablespoons soy sauce
2 teaspoons grated fresh ginger
½ teaspoon dry mustard
1 (3½-pound) chicken, cut up

1. Preheat oven to 350°F. Combine all ingredients except chicken in small bowl.

2. Place chicken in lightly greased baking dish. Brush evenly with sauce mixture. Bake 45 minutes or until cooked through (165°F), brushing occasionally with sauce.

Makes 4 to 6 servings

Orange and Maple Glazed Roast Turkey

1 small turkey (10 pounds), thawed if frozen
½ cup water
   Vegetable oil
¼ cup (½ stick) butter
½ cup orange juice
2 tablespoons maple syrup
½ teaspoon chili powder
   Salt and black pepper
1 cup chicken broth
1 to 2 teaspoons all-purpose flour

1. Preheat oven to 325°F. Remove any packets from turkey cavity.

2. Tuck ends of drumsticks into cavity; tuck tips of wings under turkey. Place on rack in shallow roasting pan; add water to pan. Brush with oil; cover loosely with heavy-duty foil. Roast 1 hour 15 minutes. Remove foil and roast, uncovered, 1 hour 15 minutes.

3. Melt butter in small saucepan over medium heat. Stir in orange juice, maple syrup, chili powder, salt and pepper; bring to a simmer. Brush turkey with glaze.

4. Roast 30 to 45 minutes or until turkey is golden brown and meat thermometer inserted into thickest part of thigh registers 165°F. Remove turkey to serving platter; cover with foil. Let stand 15 to 20 minutes before carving.

5. Skim fat from roasting pan; discard. Place roasting pan on stovetop over medium heat. Pour in ¾ cup chicken broth, scraping up browned bits on bottom of pan. Stir flour and remaining ¼ cup chicken broth in small cup until smooth. Add to roasting pan. Cook and stir over low heat until slightly thickened. If gravy is too thick, add additional broth or water. Slice turkey and serve with gravy.   *Makes 8 servings*

Porcupine Meatballs

1 tablespoon butter or margarine
1 small onion, chopped
1 pound lean ground beef*
1 cup MINUTE® White Rice, uncooked
1 egg, lightly beaten
1 small packet meatloaf seasoning
¼ cup water
1 jar (15½ ounces or larger) spaghetti sauce

Or substitute ground turkey.

Melt butter in small skillet over medium-high heat. Add onion; cook and stir until tender. Place onion, meat, rice, egg and seasoning in large bowl. Add water; mix until well blended. Shape into medium-sized meatballs. Pour spaghetti sauce into skillet. Bring to a boil. Add meatballs; return to a boil. Reduce heat to low; cover. Simmer 15 minutes or until meatballs are cooked through.   *Makes 4 servings*

Tip To quickly shape uniform meatballs, place meat mixture on cutting board and pat evenly into a large square, one-inch thick. With a sharp knife, cut meat into 1-inch squares; shape each into a ball.

Nutty Oven-Fried Chicken Drumsticks

12 chicken drumsticks (about 3 pounds)
1 egg, beaten
1 cup cornflake crumbs
⅓ cup finely chopped pecans
1 tablespoon sugar
1½ teaspoons salt
½ teaspoon onion powder
½ teaspoon black pepper
¼ cup (½ stick) butter or margarine, melted

1. Preheat oven to 400°F. Toss chicken with egg to coat.

2. Combine cornflake crumbs, pecans, sugar, salt, onion powder and pepper in large resealable food storage bag. Add chicken, two pieces at a time; shake to coat.

3. Place chicken on foil-lined baking sheet; drizzle with melted butter. Bake 40 to 45 minutes or until cooked through (165°F).   *Makes 4 to 6 servings*

Sicilian Steak Pinwheels

1¾ cups fresh bread crumbs
¾ pound mild or hot Italian sausage, casing removed
¾ cup grated Parmesan cheese
2 eggs
3 tablespoons minced parsley, plus additional for garnish
1½ to 2 pounds round steak
1 cup frozen peas
Kitchen string, cut into 15-inch lengths
1 cup pasta sauce
1 cup beef broth

Slow Cooker Directions

1. Coat slow cooker with nonstick cooking spray. Mix bread crumbs, sausage, cheese, eggs and 3 tablespoons parsley in large bowl until well blended; set aside.

2. Place round steak between 2 large sheets of plastic wrap. Pound steak using tenderizer mallet or back of skillet until meat is about ⅜ inch thick. Remove top layer of plastic wrap. Spread sausage mixture over steak. Press frozen peas into sausage mixture. Lift edge of plastic wrap at short end to begin rolling steak. Roll up completely. Tie at 2-inch intervals with kitchen string. Transfer to slow cooker.

3. Combine pasta sauce and broth in medium bowl. Pour over meat. Cover; cook on LOW 6 hours or until meat is tender and sausage is cooked through.

4. Transfer steak to serving platter. Let stand 20 minutes before removing string and slicing. Meanwhile, skim and discard excess fat from sauce. Serve steak slices with sauce.   *Makes 4 to 6 servings*

Prep Time: 20 to 25 minutes
Cook Time: 6 hours

Enchilada Slow-Roasted Baby Back Ribs

1 packet (1.25 ounces) ORTEGA® Fajita Seasoning Mix
4 tablespoons packed brown sugar
4 slabs baby back ribs (about 10 pounds)
½ cup Dijon mustard
2 jars (8 ounces each) ORTEGA® Enchilada Sauce

Preheat oven to 250°F. Combine seasoning mix and brown sugar in small bowl. Place large piece of aluminum foil on counter. On foil, brush both sides of ribs with mustard; sprinkle both sides with seasoning mixture.

Adjust one oven rack to low position. Remove remaining oven rack; arrange ribs on rack. Slide rack with ribs into upper-middle position in oven. Place foil-lined baking sheet on lower rack to collect drippings from ribs.

Roast ribs 1½ to 2 hours or until tender. Remove ribs from oven. Turn on broiler.

Brush enchilada sauce onto both sides of ribs. Transfer ribs to foil-lined baking sheet, meat side down. Broil 5 to 6 minutes or until sauce begins to bubble. Let stand 5 minutes before slicing into individual servings.   *Makes 6 to 8 servings*

Prep Time: 15 minutes
Start to Finish: 2 hours

Tip

You can also grill these ribs. Follow the same procedures, keeping the grill temperature at about 250°F and grill with the cover on.

Steak Diane with Cremini Mushrooms

Nonstick cooking spray
2 beef tenderloin steaks (4 ounces each), cut ¾ inch thick
¼ teaspoon black pepper
⅓ cup sliced shallots or chopped onion
4 ounces cremini mushrooms, sliced
1 tablespoon *each* Worcestershire sauce and Dijon mustard

1. Coat large nonstick skillet with cooking spray; heat over medium-high heat. Add steaks; sprinkle with pepper. Cook 3 minutes per side for medium-rare or desired doneness. Transfer steaks to plate; set aside.

2. Spray same skillet with cooking spray; place over medium heat. Add shallots; cook 2 minutes. Add mushrooms; cook 3 minutes, stirring frequently. Add Worcestershire sauce and mustard; cook 1 minute, stirring frequently.

3. Return steaks and any accumulated juices to skillet; heat through, turning once. Transfer steaks to serving plates; top with mushroom mixture.   *Makes 2 servings*

Turkey Wienerschnitzel

1 cup sour cream
⅔ cup plus 2 tablespoons all-purpose flour, divided
2 teaspoons paprika
1½ teaspoons salt, divided
1 egg
½ cup plus 3 tablespoons water, divided
½ teaspoon black pepper
1½ pounds boneless skinless turkey breast, pounded to ⅛-inch thickness
3 tablespoons canola or vegetable oil

1. Preheat oven to 200°F. Blend sour cream, 2 tablespoons flour, paprika and ½ teaspoon salt in small bowl; set aside.

2. Beat egg and 3 tablespoons water in large shallow dish. Combine remaining ⅔ cup flour, 1 teaspoon salt and pepper in large resealable food storage bag. Place turkey in egg mixture; turn to coat. Transfer to bag; shake to coat turkey with flour.

3. Heat oil in large skillet over medium-high heat. Shake excess flour from turkey; add to skillet. Cook until golden brown on both sides, about 4 minutes per side. Remove to ovenproof platter; place in oven to keep warm.

4. Add remaining ½ cup water to skillet; stir over medium heat, scraping up browned bits. Whisk in sour cream mixture; cook, stirring constantly, about 1 minute or until sauce is bubbly and no lumps remain. Spoon sauce over turkey.   *Makes 4 servings*

Steak Diane with Cremini Mushrooms

Southwestern Chicken and Black Bean Skillet

1 **teaspoon ground cumin**
1 **teaspoon ground chili powder**
½ **teaspoon salt**
4 **boneless skinless chicken breasts**
2 **teaspoons canola or vegetable oil**
1 **cup chopped yellow onion**
1 **red bell pepper, chopped**
1 **can (about 15 ounces) black beans, rinsed and drained**
½ **cup chunky salsa**
¼ **cup chopped fresh cilantro or thinly sliced green onion (optional)**

1. Sprinkle cumin, chili powder and salt over chicken. Heat oil in large nonstick skillet over medium-high heat. Add chicken; cook 2 minutes per side. Transfer chicken to plate; set aside.

2. Add onion to skillet; cook and stir 1 minute. Add bell pepper; cook over medium heat 5 minutes, stirring occasionally. Add beans and salsa; mix well. Place chicken over bean mixture. Cover; cook 6 to 7 minutes or until chicken is no longer pink in center. Top with cilantro.   *Makes 4 servings*

Tip   Salsa is the Spanish word for sauce. In America, it is a generic term that refers to a large, diverse group of chunky, usually highly seasoned mixtures. Salsas can be made at home from fresh ingredients or purchased. They can be based on fruits (such as papaya, mango and peaches), corn, black beans and/or vegetables.

Southwestern Chicken and Black Bean Skillet

Spicy Citrus Pork with Pineapple Salsa

1½ **teaspoons ground cumin**
½ **teaspoon coarsely ground black pepper**
¼ **teaspoon salt**
1½ **pounds center-cut pork loin, rinsed and patted dry**
1 **tablespoon vegetable oil**
2 **cans (8 ounces each) pineapple tidbits* in juice, drained, ¼ cup juice reserved, divided**
1 **teaspoon grated lemon peel**
2 **tablespoons lemon juice, divided**
½ **cup finely chopped orange or red bell pepper**
2 **tablespoons finely chopped red onion**
1 **tablespoon chopped fresh cilantro or mint**
½ **teaspoon grated fresh ginger (optional)**
⅛ **teaspoon red pepper flakes (optional)**

*If tidbits are unavailable, purchase pineapple chunks and coarsely chop.

Slow Cooker Directions

1. Coat slow cooker with nonstick cooking spray. Combine cumin, black pepper and salt in small bowl. Rub evenly onto pork. Heat oil in medium skillet over medium-high heat. Sear pork 1 to 2 minutes per side. Transfer to slow cooker.

2. Spoon 2 tablespoons reserved pineapple juice and 1 tablespoon lemon juice over pork. Cover; cook on LOW 2 hours to 2 hours 15 minutes or on HIGH 1 hour 10 minutes or until meat thermometer registers 160°F and pork is barely pink in center. *Do not overcook.*

3. Meanwhile, combine pineapple, remaining 2 tablespoons pineapple juice, lemon peel, remaining 1 tablespoon lemon juice, bell pepper, onion, cilantro, ginger and pepper flakes, if desired, in medium bowl. Toss gently to blend; set aside.

4. Transfer pork to serving platter. Let stand 10 minutes before slicing. To serve, pour sauce evenly over slices. Serve with salsa.   *Makes 6 servings*

Prep Time: 15 minutes
Cook Time: 2 hours to 2 hours 15 minutes (LOW) or 1 hour 10 minutes (HIGH)

On the Side

Twice-Baked Potatoes with Sun-Dried Tomatoes

- **4 large baking potatoes**
  Vegetable oil
- **1 container (16 ounces) sour cream**
- **2 cups (8 ounces) shredded Cheddar cheese, divided**
- **⅓ cup sun-dried tomatoes packed in oil, drained and chopped**
- **4 tablespoons finely chopped green onions, divided**
- **2 tablespoons butter, softened**
- **1 teaspoon salt**
- **½ teaspoon black pepper**

1. Preheat oven to 350°F. Scrub potatoes and pat dry with paper towels. Rub potatoes with vegetable oil; bake 1 hour. Cool 30 minutes.

2. Cut each potato in half lengthwise. Scrape potato pulp into large bowl, leaving ½-inch thick shells. Add sour cream, 1½ cups cheese, sun-dried tomatoes, 3 tablespoons green onions, butter, salt and pepper; mix gently. Fill potato shells.

3. Bake 15 to 20 minutes or until heated through. Top with remaining ½ cup cheese; bake 5 minutes or until cheese is melted. Sprinkle with remaining green onions.

Makes 8 servings

Salsa-Buttered Corn on the Cob

 6 ears fresh corn, shucked
 4 tablespoons butter, softened
 ¼ cup ORTEGA® Salsa
 2 tablespoons ORTEGA® Taco Seasoning Mix, or to taste

Bring large pot of water to a boil. Add corn; cook 5 to 10 minutes.

Combine butter and salsa in small bowl; mix well. Place seasoning mix in another small bowl. Spread salsa butter onto cooked corn and sprinkle on seasoning mix, to taste. *Makes 6 servings*

Variation: For a different side dish, cut the corn off the cob and heat in a skillet with the salsa butter and taco seasoning mix.

Prep Time: 5 minutes
Start to Finish: 20 minutes

Spinach Artichoke Gratin

 2 cups cottage cheese
 2 eggs
 4½ tablespoons grated Parmesan cheese, divided
 1 tablespoon lemon juice
 ⅛ teaspoon black pepper
 ⅛ teaspoon ground nutmeg
 2 packages (10 ounces each) frozen chopped spinach, thawed
 ⅓ cup thinly sliced green onions
 1 package (10 ounces) frozen artichoke hearts, thawed and halved

1. Preheat oven to 375°F. Coat 1½-quart baking dish with cooking spray.

2. Process cottage cheese, eggs, 3 tablespoons cheese, lemon juice, pepper and nutmeg in food processor until smooth.

3. Squeeze moisture from spinach. Combine spinach, cottage cheese mixture and green onions in large bowl. Spread half of mixture in baking dish.

4. Pat artichoke halves dry with paper towels. Place in single layer over spinach mixture. Sprinkle with remaining 1½ tablespoons cheese. Cover with remaining spinach mixture. Bake, covered, 25 minutes. *Makes 6 servings*

Green Bean Casserole

**1 can (10¾ ounces) CAMPBELL'S® Condensed Cream of Mushroom
    Soup (Regular *or* 98% Fat Free)**
½ cup milk
1 teaspoon soy sauce
    Dash ground black pepper
2 packages (10 ounces *each*) frozen cut green beans, cooked and drained
1 can (2.8 ounces) French fried onions (1⅓ cups)

1. Stir the soup, milk, soy sauce, black pepper, green beans and ⅔ cup onions in a
1½-quart casserole.

2. Bake at 350°F. for 25 minutes or until hot. Stir the green bean mixture.

3. Sprinkle the remaining onions over the green bean mixture. Bake for 5 minutes
more or until onions are golden brown.   *Makes 5 servings*

Easy Substitution: You can also make this classic side dish with fresh or canned green
beans. You will need either 1½ pounds fresh green beans, cut into 1-inch pieces,
cooked and drained or 2 cans (about 16 ounces each) cut green beans, drained for the
frozen green beans.

Start to Finish Time: 40 minutes
Prepping: 10 minutes
Baking: 30 minutes

Thyme Roasted Sweet Potatoes & Onions

2 large, unpeeled sweet potatoes (about 1¼ pounds)
2 tablespoons canola oil
1 medium sweet or yellow onion, cut into chunks
1 teaspoon dried thyme
½ teaspoon *each* salt and smoked paprika
⅛ teaspoon ground red pepper (optional)

1. Preheat oven to 425°F. Coat 15×10-inch jelly-roll pan with nonstick cooking
spray.

2. Cut sweet potatoes into 1-inch chunks; place in large bowl. Add oil; toss well. Add
onion, thyme, salt, paprika and red pepper, if desired; toss well.

3. Spread vegetables in single layer on prepared pan. Bake 20 to 25 minutes or until
very tender, stirring after 10 minutes. Let stand 5 minutes before serving.
                    Makes 10 servings

Chunky Ranch Potatoes

    3 pounds medium red potatoes, unpeeled and quartered
    1 cup water
    ½ cup prepared ranch dressing
    ½ cup grated Parmesan or Cheddar cheese (optional)
    ¼ cup minced chives

Slow Cooker Directions

1. Place potatoes in slow cooker. Add water. Cover; cook on LOW 7 to 9 hours or on HIGH 4 to 6 hours or until potatoes are tender.

2. Stir in ranch dressing, cheese, if desired, and chives. Use spoon to break up potatoes into chunks. Serve hot or cold.   *Makes 8 servings*

Prep Time: 10 minutes
Cook Time: 7 to 9 hours (LOW) or 4 to 6 hours (HIGH)

Glazed Parsnips and Carrots

    1 pound parsnips
    8 ounces baby carrots
    1 tablespoon canola oil
      Salt and black pepper
    ¼ cup orange juice
    1 tablespoon unsalted butter or margarine
    1 tablespoon honey
    ⅛ teaspoon ground ginger

1. Preheat oven to 425°F. Peel parsnips; cut into wedges the same size as baby carrots.

2. Spread vegetables in shallow roasting pan. Drizzle with oil and sprinkle with salt and pepper; toss to coat. Bake 30 to 35 minutes or until fork-tender.

3. Combine orange juice, butter, honey and ginger in large skillet. Add roasted vegetables; cook and stir over high heat 1 to 2 minutes, stirring frequently, until sauce thickens and coats vegetables. Season with additional salt and pepper, if desired.
          Makes 6 servings

Fennel Braised with Tomato

2 bulbs fennel
1 tablespoon olive oil
1 small onion, sliced
1 clove garlic, sliced
4 medium tomatoes, chopped
⅔ cup plus 3 tablespoons vegetable broth
1 tablespoon chopped fresh marjoram *or* **1 teaspoon dried marjoram**
¼ teaspoon salt
¼ teaspoon black pepper

1. Trim stems and bottoms of fennel bulbs, reserving green leafy tops for garnish. Cut each bulb lengthwise into 4 wedges.

2. Heat oil in large skillet over medium heat. Cook fennel, onion and garlic, stirring occasionally, until onion is soft and translucent, about 5 minutes.

3. Add tomatoes, broth and marjoram. Season with salt and pepper. Cover; simmer gently until fennel is tender, about 20 minutes. Garnish with fennel leaves.

Makes 6 servings

Garlic and Chipotle Cheddar Mashed Potatoes

5 pounds russet potatoes, peeled and cut into 1-inch pieces
36 cloves garlic, roasted*
1¾ cups (7 ounces) SARGENTO® Bistro® Blends Shredded Chipotle Cheddar Cheese
4 ounces cream cheese, room temperature
¼ cup (½ stick) unsalted butter, room temperature

*To roast garlic, slice tops off each of three bulbs. Drizzle with ⅓ cup olive oil. Roast at 400°F for 45 minutes. Cool. Reserve garlic oil for another use. Squeeze garlic cloves from skins.

Cook potatoes in large pot of boiling salted water until tender, about 25 minutes. Drain. Add garlic, cheeses and butter. Mash mixture until smooth. Season to taste with salt and pepper.

Makes 8 servings

Ham Seasoned Peas

    1 teaspoon olive oil
    ¼ pound cooked ham, chopped
    ¼ cup chopped onion
    2 cups (about 9 ounces) frozen peas
    ¼ cup chicken broth
    ⅛ to ¼ teaspoon dried oregano
    ⅛ teaspoon black pepper (optional)

1. Heat oil in medium saucepan. Add ham and onion; cook until onion is translucent.

2. Stir in peas, broth, oregano and pepper, if desired. Bring to a boil. Reduce heat; simmer, covered, 4 to 5 minutes or until peas are tender.   *Makes 4 servings*

Prep Time: 5 minutes
Cook Time: 10 minutes

Spanish Stewed Tomatoes

    2 tablespoons olive oil
    ½ teaspoon POLANER® Chopped Garlic
    1 can (15 ounces) diced tomatoes
    ½ cup water
    1 packet (1.25 ounces) ORTEGA® Taco Seasoning Mix
    2 cups frozen green beans
    2 tablespoons ORTEGA® Diced Green Chiles

Heat oil in medium skillet over medium heat until hot. Add garlic. Cook and stir until golden brown. Stir in tomatoes, water and seasoning mix. Simmer 3 minutes. Add beans and chiles; simmer 4 minutes longer or until beans are heated through.

Makes 6 servings

Variation: Replace the green beans with corn or lima beans.

Prep Time: 5 minutes
Start to Finish: 15 minutes

Creamy Golden Mushroom Mashed Potatoes

6 medium baking potatoes, cut into 1-inch pieces (about 6 cups)
1 small onion, cut into wedges
  Water
1 can (10¾ ounces) CAMPBELL'S® Condensed Golden Mushroom Soup
¾ cup milk
¼ cup heavy cream
4 tablespoons butter

1. Put the potatoes and onion in a 4-quart saucepot with enough water to cover them. Heat the potatoes over medium-high heat to a boil. Reduce the heat to low. Cover and cook the potatoes for 20 minutes or until fork-tender. Drain the potatoes and onion well in a colander.

2. Put the potatoes and onion in a 3-quart bowl and beat with an electric mixer at medium speed until almost smooth.

3. Put the soup, milk, cream and butter in a 4-cup microwavable measuring cup. Microwave on HIGH for 2½ minutes or until hot. Slowly pour the hot soup mixture into the potatoes, beating with an electric mixer at medium speed until the potatoes are smooth. Season to taste. *Makes 6 servings*

Start to Finish Time: 50 minutes
Prep Time: 20 minutes
Cook Time: 30 minutes

Creamy Spinach-Stuffed Portobellos

    4 large portobello mushrooms
    1 tablespoon vegetable oil
    1 medium onion, chopped (about ½ cup)
    1 medium tomato, chopped (about 1 cup)
    1 bag (6 ounces) baby spinach leaves, washed
    1 can (10¾ ounces) CAMPBELL'S® Condensed Cream of Celery Soup
        (Regular *or* 98% Fat Free)
    2 tablespoons grated Parmesan cheese
    1 tablespoon dry bread crumbs, toasted

1. Remove the stems from the mushrooms. Set the caps top side down in 13×9×2-inch baking pan.

2. Heat the oil in a 10-inch nonstick skillet over medium heat. Add the onion and cook until the onion is tender-crisp. Add the tomato and spinach; cook just until the spinach is wilted. Stir in the soup and heat through.

3. Spoon the filling into the mushroom caps.

4. Bake at 425°F. for 15 minutes or until mushrooms are hot.

5. Mix the cheese with bread crumbs in a small cup. Sprinkle over the mushrooms.

6. Heat the broiler. Broil the mushrooms with the top of the mushrooms 4 inches from the heat for about 5 minutes or until topping is golden.   *Makes 4 servings*

Start to Finish Time: 30 minutes
Prepping: 10 minutes
Baking/Broiling Time: 20 minutes

Almond and Vanilla Green Beans

    1½ pounds fresh green beans, trimmed
    ⅓ cup sliced almonds
    ¼ cup (½ stick) butter
    2½ teaspoons WATKINS® Vanilla Extract
        Salt and WATKINS® Black Pepper, to taste

Cook beans until crisp-tender; drain well and keep warm. Cook and stir almonds in butter until golden brown. Remove from heat; stir in vanilla, salt and pepper. Pour over beans; serve hot.   *Makes 9 servings*

Chutney Glazed Carrots

2 cups carrots, cut into 1½-inch pieces
3 tablespoons cranberry or mango chutney
1 tablespoon Dijon mustard
2 teaspoons butter
2 tablespoons chopped pecans, toasted*

*To toast pecans, spread in single layer on ungreased baking sheet. Bake in preheated 350°F oven 5 to 7 minutes or until fragrant, stirring occasionally.

1. Place carrots in medium saucepan; cover with water. Bring to a boil over high heat. Reduce heat; simmer 6 to 8 minutes or until carrots are tender.

2. Drain carrots; return to pan. Add chutney, mustard and butter. Cook, stirring constantly, over medium heat about 2 minutes or until carrots are glazed. Top with pecans.   *Makes 4 servings*

Prep Time: 5 minutes
Cook Time: 10 minutes

Candied Sweet Potatoes

MAZOLA PURE® Cooking Spray
1 can (29 ounces) cut sweet potatoes, drained
3 tablespoons butter or margarine
½ cup KARO® Light or Dark Corn Syrup
3 tablespoons sugar
¾ teaspoon salt
¾ teaspoon ground cinnamon

1. Coat shallow 1½- to 2-quart baking dish with cooking spray. Place sweet potatoes in prepared dish.

2. In small saucepan over low heat melt butter. Stir in corn syrup, sugar, salt and cinnamon. Cook and stir 1 to 2 minutes or until smooth. Pour evenly over sweet potatoes; stir gently to coat.

3. Bake in 350°F oven 20 minutes or until hot and bubbly.

Makes 4 to 6 servings

Prep Time: 10 minutes
Cook Time: 20 minutes

Delicious Desserts

Chocolate Vanilla Swirl Cheesecake

- 20 OREO® Chocolate Sandwich Cookies, crushed (about 2 cups)
- 3 tablespoons butter, melted
- 4 packages (8 ounces each) PHILADELPHIA® Cream Cheese, softened
- 1 cup sugar
- 1 teaspoon vanilla
- 1 cup BREAKSTONE'S® or KNUDSEN® Sour Cream
- 4 eggs
- 6 squares BAKER'S® Semi-Sweet Baking Chocolate, melted, cooled

PREHEAT oven to 325°F. Line 13×9-inch baking pan with foil, with ends of foil extending over sides of pan. Mix cookie crumbs and butter; press firmly onto bottom of prepared pan. Bake 10 minutes.

BEAT cream cheese, sugar and vanilla in large bowl with electric mixer on medium speed until well blended. Add sour cream; mix well. Add eggs, 1 at a time, beating on low speed after each addition just until blended. Remove 1 cup of the batter; set aside. Stir melted chocolate into remaining batter. Pour chocolate batter over crust; top with spoonfuls of remaining plain batter. Cut through batters with knife several times for swirled effect.

BAKE 40 minutes or until center is almost set. Cool. Refrigerate at least 4 hours or overnight. Use foil handles to lift cheesecake from pan before cutting to serve. Store any leftover cheesecake in refrigerator.   *Makes 16 servings, 1 piece each*

Prep Time: 15 minutes plus refrigerating
Bake Time: 40 minutes

Tip: Jazz It Up! Garnish with chocolate curls just before serving. Use a vegetable peeler to shave the side of an additional square of BAKER'S® Semi-Sweet Baking Chocolate and a square of BAKER'S® Premium White Baking Chocolate until desired amount of curls are obtained. Wrap remaining chocolate and store at room temperature for another use.

Carrot Cake with Black Walnut Frosting

1 cup granulated sugar
3 eggs
⅔ cup WATKINS® Original Grapeseed Oil
1 teaspoon WATKINS® Vanilla
1½ cups all-purpose flour
2 teaspoons WATKINS® Ground Cinnamon
½ teaspoon WATKINS® Ground Cloves
½ teaspoon WATKINS® Nutmeg
½ teaspoon WATKINS® Allspice
1½ teaspoons baking soda
1 teaspoon WATKINS® Baking Powder
½ teaspoon salt
2 cups finely grated carrots
1 cup walnuts, chopped
1 package (8 ounces) cream cheese
⅓ cup butter, at room temperature
½ teaspoon WATKINS® Vanilla Nut Extract
½ teaspoon WATKINS® Butter Pecan or Vanilla Nut Extract
2½ cups powdered sugar

Preheat oven to 350°F. Spray two 9×2-inch round pans with WATKINS® Cooking Spray; dust with flour. Combine granulated sugar, eggs and oil in large bowl; beat for 1 minute. Stir in vanilla. Add flour, spices, baking soda, baking powder and salt; beat about 1 minute. Fold in carrots and walnuts. Pour into prepared pans. Bake for 30 minutes or until toothpick inserted into center comes out clean.

Beat cream cheese, butter and extracts in medium bowl until smooth. Add powdered sugar, ½ cup at a time; beat until frosting is of spreading consistency. Fill and frost cake.   *Makes 12 servings*

Variations: Add golden raisins or pineapple to batter, if desired. Or substitute 2 cups shredded zucchini for the shredded carrots.

Cherry Crisp

1 **(21-ounce) can cherry pie filling**
½ **teaspoon almond extract**
½ **cup all-purpose flour**
½ **cup firmly packed brown sugar**
1 **teaspoon ground cinnamon**
3 **tablespoons butter or margarine, softened**
½ **cup chopped walnuts**
¼ **cup flaked coconut**
   Ice cream or whipped cream (optional)

Pour cherry pie filling into ungreased 8×8×2-inch baking pan. Stir in almond extract.

Place flour, brown sugar and cinnamon in medium mixing bowl; mix well. Add butter; stir with fork until mixture is crumbly. Stir in walnuts and coconut. Sprinkle mixture over cherry pie filling.

Bake in preheated 350°F oven 25 minutes or until golden brown on top and filling is bubbly. Serve warm or at room temperature. If desired, top with ice cream or whipped cream.   *Makes 6 servings*

Note: This recipe can be doubled. Bake in two 8×8×2-inch baking pans or one 13×9×2-inch pan.

Favorite recipe from **Cherry Marketing Institute**

HERSHEY®S Brownies with Peanut Butter Frosting

½ cup (1 stick) butter or margarine
4 sections (½ ounce each) HERSHEY®S Unsweetened Chocolate
    Premium Baking Bar, broken into pieces
1 cup sugar
2 eggs
1 teaspoon vanilla extract
½ cup all-purpose flour
¼ teaspoon baking powder
¼ teaspoon salt
½ cup chopped nuts
    Peanut Butter Frosting (optional)

1. Heat oven to 350°F. Grease 8-inch square baking pan.

2. Melt butter and chocolate in medium saucepan over low heat. Remove from heat; stir in sugar. Beat in eggs and vanilla with wooden spoon. Stir together flour, baking powder and salt. Add to chocolate mixture, blending well. Stir in nuts. Pour batter into prepared pan.

3. Bake 30 to 35 minutes or until brownies begin to pull away from sides of pan. Cool completely in pan on wire rack. Frost with Peanut Butter Frosting, if desired. Cut into squares. *Makes about 16 brownies*

Peanut Butter Frosting

1 cup powdered sugar
¼ cup REESE'S® Creamy Peanut Butter
2 tablespoons milk
½ teaspoon vanilla extract

1. Combine all ingredients in small bowl; beat until smooth. If necessary, add additional milk, ½ teaspoon at a time, until of desired consistency.

Makes about ¾ cup frosting

New York-Style Sour Cream-Topped Cheesecake

1½ cups HONEY MAID® Graham Cracker Crumbs
¼ cup (½ stick) butter, melted
1¼ cups sugar, divided
4 packages (8 ounces each) PHILADELPHIA® Cream Cheese, softened
2 teaspoons vanilla, divided
1 container (16 ounces) BREAKSTONE'S® or KNUDSEN® Sour Cream, divided
4 eggs

PREHEAT oven to 325°F. Line 13×9-inch baking pan with foil, with ends of foil extending over sides of pan. Mix crumbs, butter and 2 tablespoons of the sugar; press firmly onto bottom of prepared pan.

BEAT cream cheese, 1 cup of the remaining sugar and 1 teaspoon of the vanilla in large bowl with electric mixer on medium speed until well blended. Add 1 cup of the sour cream; mix well. Add eggs, one at a time, beating on low speed after each addition just until blended. Pour over crust.

BAKE 40 minutes or until center is almost set. Mix remaining sour cream, 2 tablespoons sugar and 1 teaspoon vanilla until well blended; carefully spread over cheesecake. Bake an additional 10 minutes. Cool. Cover; refrigerate 4 hours or overnight. Lift cheesecake from pan using foil handles. Garnish as desired. Store leftover cheesecake in refrigerator.   *Makes 16 servings, 1 piece each*

Substitution: Prepare as directed, substituting 1½ cups finely crushed OREO® Chocolate Sandwich Cookies for the graham cracker crumbs.

Prep Time: 15 minutes plus refrigerating
Bake Time: 40 minutes

Tip   To prevent cracking, do not overmix the cheesecake batter; beat just until the mixture is blended.

Pumpkin Custard

1 **cup solid-pack pumpkin**
½ **cup packed brown sugar**
2 **eggs, beaten**
½ **teaspoon ground ginger**
½ **teaspoon grated lemon peel**
½ **teaspoon ground cinnamon, plus additional for topping**
1 **can (12 ounces) evaporated milk**
Additional ground cinnamon

Slow Cooker Directions

1. Combine pumpkin, brown sugar, eggs, ginger, lemon peel and ½ teaspoon cinnamon in large bowl. Stir in evaporated milk. Pour mixture into 1½-quart soufflé dish. Cover tightly with foil.

2. Make foil handles.* Place soufflé dish in slow cooker. Pour water into 4½-quart slow cooker to come about 1½ inches from top of soufflé dish. Cover; cook on LOW 4 hours.

3. Use foil handles to lift dish from slow cooker. Sprinkle with additional ground cinnamon. Serve warm.   *Makes 6 servings*

To make foil handles, tear off three 18×3-inch strips of heavy-duty foil. Crisscross the strips so they resemble the spokes of a wheel. Place the dish in the center of the strips. Pull the foil strips up and over dish. Place in the slow cooker. Leave them in while you cook so you can easily lift the dish out again when ready.

The publisher would like to thank the companies and organizations listed below for the use of their recipes and photographs in this publication.

ACH Food Companies, Inc.

Campbell Soup Company

Cherry Marketing Institute

The Hershey Company

©2010 Kraft Foods, KRAFT, KRAFT Hexagon Logo, PHILADELPHIA AND PHILADELPHIA Logo are registered trademarks of Kraft Foods Holdings, Inc. All rights reserved.

McIlhenny Company (TABASCO® brand Pepper Sauce)

Nestlé USA

Ortega®, A Division of B&G Foods, Inc.

Reckitt Benckiser Inc.

Riviana Foods Inc.

Roman Meal® Company

Sargento® Foods Inc.

Sonoma® Dried Tomatoes

Watkins Incorporated